811
DOBYNS, STEPHEN
HEAT DEATH   ($5.95)

3

(

WAYNE PUBLIC LIBRARY

MAIN LIBRARY

475 Valley Road

Wayne, N. J. 07470

Books may be returned at any
branch of the library.

DEC 1 1980

D1570860

Heat Death

Books by Stephen Dobyns

POEMS

Heat Death   1980
Griffon   1976
Concurring Beasts   1972

NOVELS

Saratoga Longshot   1976
A Man of Little Evils   1973

Heat Death

Poems by Stephen Dobyns

New York 1980 Atheneum

Acknowledgements are due to the editors of the following publications for permission to reprint poems in this book.

IOWA REVIEW: "Fragments," "Song of the Wrong Response."

IRONWOOD: "The Body of Romulus."

KAYAK: "Night Song," "The Poem As Actor In Three Parts For Michael Ryan," "Song of the Drowned Boy," "Song of Four Dancers."

MISSOURI REVIEW: "Geese," "Snow."

THE NEW YORKER: "The Delicate, Plummeting Bodies," "Getting Through Winter," "Rain Song."

NORTH AMERICAN REVIEW: "Pablo Neruda."

PEQUOD: "Discoveries," "Footstep," "Letter Beginning With The First Line Of Your Letter," "Moon Song," "The Photographs," "Song For Falling Asleep," "Winter Branches."

PLOUGHSHARES: "Separations."

POETRY: "A Place In Maine," "Arrested Saturday Night," "A Separate Time," "How Sweet And Proper It Is," "It's Like This," "Morning Song," "Oatmeal Deluxe," "Song For Making The Birds Come," "Song For Putting Aside Anger."

TENDRIL: "In Place Of A Letter," "Street At Sannois."

VIRGINIA QUARTERLY REVIEW: "Fear," "Song Of Basic Necessities."

Thanks are also due to the Corporation of Yaddo and MacDowell Colony where a number of these poems were written.

Copyright © 1977, 1978, 1979, 1980 by Stephen Dobyns
All rights reserved
Published simultaneously in Canada by McClelland and Stewart Ltd
Library of Congress catalog card number 79-55592
ISBN 0-689-11034-0 (clothbound); ISBN 0-689-11063-4 (paperback)
Manufactured by American Book-Stratford Press, Saddle Brook, New Jersey
Designed by Kathleen Carey
First Edition

for Rebecca

Contents

Heat Death

Rain Song

for Mekeel

The woods are full of men with umbrellas—
the butcher from Roy's Market, the mechanic
who fixed my car— they are looking for you.
They heard of a woman lying naked in the fields:
that was you. For days you lay in the north pasture
to encourage spring, as the sun touched your thighs,
your belly and breasts, and was at last so
disconcerted that the sky clouded over
and the president of rain took you for his wife.
You wore blue to the wedding; even the crows sang.
Now, hurrying through the trees, the black umbrellas
do not realize it is you dripping from juniper
and birch, forming puddles, then rivulets and
running downhill to the river flowing through town.
The people of Peterborough bathe in your body.
They drink glass after glass and say they feel better.
They smash their televisions and prepare to go dancing.
The fat town clerk and tax consultant, legions
of Republicans removing their clothes, baton twirlers
and firemen's band— all march naked through the street,
banging cymbals and drums as you touch them,
blowing their horns as you run down their backs,
tumbling at last into lascivious piles on this
rainy Sunday they will long remember but which you
have already forgotten as you flow down to the sea
into the stories of sailors and promiscuous fish,
and past that small promontory where I stand,
body greased and waiting for the long swim.

Street at Sannois

(AFTER UTRILLO)

Bordered by white walls, the road curves north
up the hill before disappearing among the pines.
It's early evening and the sky is dark blue.
Two white houses with red shutters face each other
across the road: flush against the sidewalk, flush
within the wall. For years the families of these houses
have suspected and envied each other until each
is now the image of the other's boredom and defeat.
Tonight the house on the left is empty except for
a servant drying dishes. As she works, she listens
to the talk of couples passing in the street,
while through the window come the smells of October:
dry wind and smoke from where a neighbor is burning
the last of his garden. As she places the blue
dishes in the cupboard, the girl comes to consider
the warm rooms of winter, then spring with first
crocuses nudging the black soil. For a moment,
in this taste of air, she forgets the plates and
polishing of silver that nobody uses, and in
the unfolding of the year she finds only possibility,
while all her common fears— death in childbirth,
murder in the night— become as nearly invisible
as the open window dividing her from the street.
She completes her work and folds her apron. Shortly
she will pass through the gate, greeting her neighbors,
and as a glass fills with water so she will fill
with the wonder that this night and each day to come
are as soft and enveloping as the blue gloves which
she is just now tugging over her small, rough hands.

4

Oatmeal Deluxe

This morning, because the snow swirled deep
around my house, I made oatmeal for breakfast.
At first it was runny so I added more oatmeal,
then it grew too thick so I added water.
Soon I had a lot of oatmeal. The radio
was playing Spanish music and I became
passionate: soon I had four pots of oatmeal.
I put them aside and started a new batch.
Soon I had eight pots. When the oatmeal cooled,
I began to roll it with my hands, making
small shapes: pigs and souvenir ashtrays. Then
I made a foot, then another, then a leg. Soon
I'd made a woman out of oatmeal with freckles
and a cute nose and hair made from brown sugar
and naked except for a necklace of raisins.
She was five feet long and when she grew harder
I could move her arms and legs without them
falling off. But I didn't touch her much—
she lay on the table— sometimes I'd touch her
with a spoon, sometimes I'd lick her in places
it wouldn't show. She looks like you, although
your hair is darker, but the smile is like yours,
and the eyes, although hers are closed. You say:
But what has this to do with me? And I should say:
I want to make more women from Cream of Wheat.
But enough of such fantasy. You ask me
why I don't love you, why you can't
live with me. What can I tell you? If I
can make a woman out of oatmeal, my friend,
what trouble could I make for you, a woman?

How Sweet and Proper It Is

Color of silver, surrounded by barbed wire,
the tower rises from the hill like a thumb
from a fist. A young man climbs from his horse,
begins to crawl through the wire toward a door
at the base of the tower. His clothing and skin
are torn but that is partly what he came for.
Finding the door locked, he further bruises his body
by breaking it down. Then he begins to climb.
Who would have thought bats so plentiful?
At the top of the stairs he finds a round chamber
and he's so excited he doesn't notice the men
sleeping on the floor. He only sees the woman
arranged neatly on the stone couch. She even looks
stonelike and her white dress seems stonelike
and she has the face of statues on public buildings:
justice or civic virtue. The young man knows little
but what he knows convinces him that she's beautiful.
He runs toward her, but in his eagerness he doesn't
see the movement of eyes beneath lids, the slight
fluttering of the lashes. He doesn't ask himself
why she's there or what his role must be: whether
as an actor in some Freudian joke or in a fable
about what it means to serve the state. Reaching her,
he presses his lips to hers, feels the coldness
of stone, feels his own body's warmth drain from him.
Then, rising, he's exhausted and he tells himself
he must catch his breath and he takes his place
among the others on the floor who he is just now
coming to notice.

Shortly, a second man appears
at the top of the stairs, and his clothing and skin
are torn but that is partly what he came for.
And he's so excited he doesn't hear the snoring,
but runs toward the woman on the stone couch.
Outside a third man pauses by the barbed wire,
while miles away another steps from his front door,
looks at the blue sky and spring birds fluttering
from maple to oak, and he decides to saddle his horse.
Perhaps he can find some quest, something to make
a name for himself, and climbing into the saddle
he stares off across the hills and far away he sees
the flicker of some silver thing, perhaps beckoning.

Song of the Drowned Boy

Three oranges on a blue plate,
black loveseat on the cropped grass:
curlicues of iron; August afternoon,
small white clouds; pond surrounded
by a ring of birch, white rowboat half up
on the shore, clothes folded in the bow;
white hand below the surface of the water—
in the distance someone is calling;
fish break the surface, ever expanding circles;
a crow caws three times and is gone.

Lady of darkness wants a fair child;
Lady of cold needs someone to warm her;
Lady of water has taken me home.

Winter Branches

Against the twilit sky, the winter branches
pin and transfix the rectangle of light outside
the window, seeming to hold it immobile. In bed,
where he's been sent as punishment for something
he can hardly remember, the boy, holding his knees,
imagines picking a path between twigs and sticks
stuck like so many swords through a magician's box.
The hall door is open and from downstairs he hears
his parents talking in the room where the fireplace
has been sealed over and painted white to keep something
in or out, he's never sure which. Now, climbing from bed,
the boy puts on his clothes, shoes, then quietly
descends the carpeted stairs. The living room door
is a square of light and the voices, although he
can't hear the words, sound comfortable and soothing.
He wants to run into the room, laughing and surprising
the adults, but instead he puts on his coat, opens
the front door to the porch. The street is empty and
from nearby houses lights shine in kitchen windows
in this hour before dinner. Running toward the woods
through the backyard, the boy passes under trees where
hundreds of sparrows settling for the night chatter
and rustle in the last light of the sun. Looking back,
the boy sees the lights of his own house, but instead
of returning he enters the woods, taking a path along
the low ridge with a tangle of brambles on either side.

He walks faster, then begins to run. His unbuttoned
blue parka flaps open and he feels the cold stiffen
the insides of his nose, lie like a flat metal strip
back of his tongue. He runs faster and lifts his arms.
The path is a straight line and rising up at the end
a crescent moon curves like a red mouth until it seems
to press itself against the opening between the trees.

Nearby in a slight hollow to the left of the path
three older boys huddle around a fire preparing
their dinner. They think themselves bold and ready
for trouble. One looks up and through the cross-hatching
of winter branches he notices a boy in a blue parka
rushing along the path, hears him making a noise
like wind pushing through a crack in a door, sees
the moon's lopsided grin hanging among the trees
and the boy running toward it as if he meant to
hurl himself against it. The older boy watches,
but then, not caring, he turns back to his friends
who have just skinned a squirrel which they intend
to roast on a spit over the fire: a pointed stick
rammed through it from one end to the other.

Discoveries

Grown stiff his hands discover
the resiliency of objects. He touches
chairs, books, and enters his rooms
like trying on the clothing of strangers:
nothing is comfortable or known.
With him now is the shape of his death:
a smaller person ever beside him.
He sees it as a child kept in
as punishment for a mistake nearly
forgiven. Soon it will leave his house,
run out to a lawn bordered
with yellow narcissus where the grass
is just cut and a new day beginning.

The Body of Romulus

The granular surface of the snow shines like parchment
in the afternoon sun as we stand on a hill above
Lake McBride. Beneath us several red snowmobiles
race across the ice. Parts seem unfrozen and we keep
pausing in our argument to wonder why the machines
don't plunge through into the December water.
For hours we argue about history which you say
is simply the story of great names and ignores
those others who suffered to keep them fed. But later
in Plutarch I read of Romulus and how one day he was
haranguing his people in a place called Goat's Marsh
when a storm over-took the sky turning day to night
and how people fled and the senators grouped together.
When the storm passed, Romulus had disappeared and
the senators claimed he'd been lifted body and soul
directly into heaven. One even swore he had seen
Romulus taller and more beautiful than before, dressed
in flaming armor, and that Romulus told him he was
departing from Rome to become a god and henceforward
he should be worshipped under the name Quirinus.
But Plutarch tells us that while the soul of a good man
is like dry light which flies from the body as lightning
breaks from a cloud, and while the soul of a wicked man
rises from the body like heavy incense, it is wrong
to think body and soul can be transported together
into heaven. Instead he argues that after Romulus
won his battles and established his city he became as
all men do who are raised by good fortune to greatness,

that he gave up popular behavior for kingly arrogance,
that he no longer maintained his office but dressed
in scarlet with the purple-bordered robe over it
and that he surrounded himself with young men
with clubs who carried thongs of leather to bind up
whomever Romulus commanded. And Plutarch suggests
that when the sky turned black with terrible
thunderings and boisterous winds from all quarters,
and when people fled and the men with clubs fled,
then the senators grouped around Romulus and slew him
and cut up his body and each carried away a small
piece in his bosom while rain carried away the blood.
And tonight after a day of argument I write this to say
that although the great names of history are given words
in books for you to believe or disbelieve as you choose,
to all the others are given the body of Romulus.
For Plutarch wrote that whoever becomes a despot becomes
contemptible, and wherever this may happen, even here
in this small Iowa town where the houses are like rows
of garden vegetables and sleep is an official sport,
even here the small names will trickle into the street
like small drops of water, and with them they will carry
tokens from the past: perfectly shaped fingers, bone,
pieces of liver, the bright blue eyes of the god.

A Separate Time

In the years since I saw you on Sunday,
I left my home and walked out across the earth
with only my occasional luck and knowledge of cards.
I met men and women constantly dissatisfied,
who hadn't learned to close their hands,
who sewed and patched their few words
fashioning garments they hoped to grow into.
There were winters sheltered in a cabin beneath pines.
There were frozen rivers and animals crazy with hunger.
But always I saw myself walking toward you,
as a drop of water touching the earth immediately
turns toward the sea. Tonight I visit your house.
In the time precious to newspapers and clocks,
only a few days have passed. The room is quiet.
Looking into your eyes, I become like the exile
who turns the corner of the last cliff and suddenly
looks down into the valley of his homeland,
sees the terraced fields and white-roofed houses
gathered on the hillside: then, the smell of woodsmoke
and a woman calling her husband in for the night.

Getting Through Winter

A white jacket and white summer dress,
dark hat with a clear veil, green parasol
set against the sky— I imagine you like this,
standing amid yellow foxglove and buttercup
at the top of a small rise. You are directly
between me and the sun, giving the edges
of your dress and veil the transparency
of insects' wings, white water over a falls.
The movements of your face become metaphor
for summer fields beyond this hill, as wisps
of sunlit cloud are metaphors for your body.
You look toward me and your shadow approaches
so close that I begin to reach out, except
that this is a picture and I am alone in my
small house, wrapped by winter fog as a wound
is wrapped by its bandage. If this could be
an actual picture, then I would attach copies
to all the windows of my weather-soaked house;
then, wherever I looked, it would be summer,
and emerging from this night I would become like
some plant that turns east each morning or
like some songless bird when the sun crests
the edge of its green world, and over and over
it attempts to pronounce its few cracked notes.

Song for Making the Birds Come

for Shirley Stark

All winter you felt nothing. As your body
continued its necessary tasks, your sister,
the snow, remained keeper of your heart.
Now it's the first warm day of spring.
You walk out to the pasture. There's much mud,
and still snow on the north side by the pines.
You take this poem from your pocket.
Raising your voice, you read it aloud to the sky.
Soon birds begin to come, first the dark ones:
birds of anger, birds of despair. Then you see
the wren of friendship, the gray dove of hope;
then others of patience, joy and love's own red bird.
As you read, they begin to fill the air above you,
twisting and diving in great circles around you;
covering the poem with the sound of their cries
until poem and song become the same sound,
blending together under the warm March sun.
At last you emerge from the apathy of winter.
Your heart is a great tree beginning to bud.
In narrowing spirals, careful descent, the birds
you have summoned arrive to make their nests.

Morning Song

Today, the pastures have dressed in their best grasses
      to parade past my window. They dress for you.
      Wake and choose among them.

Today, the sky which has been skittish all month, ducking
      behind clouds, seems to pulsate as the vein
      in your neck now pulsates when I lay one finger
      against it.

Today, the air, gathered in damp clumps, begins
      flickering with a blue light and there's a smell
      like a transformer gone bad; the hum of something
      at its dinner; the hum my bones make when you touch me.

Today, the snow which has turned a shade grayer each day
      contracts into a startlingly white cube, ten feet
      by ten feet, which strangers are already arriving
      to photograph. Sometimes your smile is so white,
      sometimes the white areas of your eyes.

Today, waking beside you, I saw the day had brought
      its best sky, air and circumstances to my house
      at the bottom of blue sky, and it seemed all this
      grew from your own white belly, and that I was like
      a poor gardener who stares up at immense scarlet
      flowers where he had thought to plant tomatoes,
      who stares at his hands, keeps turning them over,
      keeps glancing doubtfully over his shoulder,
      not knowing for what.

Fear

His life frightened him. The sun in the sky,
the man next door— they all frightened him.
Fear became a brown dog that followed him home.
Instead of driving it away, he became its friend.
The brown dog named fear followed him everywhere.
When he looked in the mirror, he saw it under
his reflection. When he talked to strangers,
he heard it growl in their voices. He had a wife:
fear chased her away. He had several friends:
fear drove them from his home. The dog fear
fed upon his heart. He was too frightened
to die, too frightened to leave the house.
Fear gnawed a cave in his chest where it
shivered and whined in the night. Wherever
he went, the dog found him, until he became
no more than a bone in its mouth, until fear
fixed its collar around his throat, fixed
its leash to the collar. The dog named fear
became the only creature he could count on.
He learned to fetch the sticks it threw for him,
eat at the dish fear filled for him. See him
on the street, seemingly lost, nose pressed
against the heel of fear. See him in his backyard,
barking at the moon. It is his own face he
finds there, hopeless and afraid, and he leaps at it,
over and over, biting and rending the night air.

Night Song

The day darkens. You have not
light enough to push the night
from your rooms. In your mirror,
you see an older self just returned
from a country where you are going.
As you watch him, you imagine
a vast plain under a lowering sky.
There are no stars, but in the distance
are sparse fires of memory, and regret
like an animal's call on the night air.
He has returned through a place as cold
as indifference or an empty heart,
and you would ask some question,
but he brings neither help nor comfort,
offers no message but silence. So you
step aside. You think this was not
what you were promised or even
planned for. What plans, what had you
intended? You fall like a pebble flicked
from a window above a darkening street.

The Photographs

for Roswell Angier

Turning within him moment by
moment separate lives which
through his life he tries to
give name to or simply discover
on the street for instance when
from shop windows he is the only one
to return his glance or in early
morning as first birds describe
the day and he says may I not be
that one, not that one, or this moment
as the photographer arranges the world
around him and he turns like ducks on
a shooting-gallery wheel and the camera
clicks once and once again: refugees from
the village of self, first the barefoot,
those with empty hands; then the rich,
each with a gold tooth, one tin spoon.

Fragments

for D.M.

Now there is a slit in the blue fabric of air.
His house spins faster. He holds down books,
chairs; his life and its objects fly upward:
vanishing black specks in the indifferent sky.

The sky is a torn piece of blue paper.
He tries to repair it, but the memory
of death is like paste on his fingers
and certain days stick like dead flies.

Say the sky goes back to being the sky
and the sun continues as always. Now, knowing
what you know, how can you not see thin
cracks in the fragile blue vaults of air?

My friend, what can I give you or darkness
lift from you but fragments of language,
fragments of blue sky. You had three
beautiful daughters and one has died.

Footstep

Each evening the man whose wife has gone
reads the paper with his back to the window.
She died in winter: cancer or a car sliding
wildly out of control— the cause doesn't matter.
At the hour when she often came home,
he begins hearing the footsteps of neighbors
passing in front of the house. Sometimes
one pauses, and briefly on the page before him
he sees her face as she looked on returning
from work or the store: cheerful and expectant.
The room trembles with possibility. Then the fact
of her death strikes him and once more she dies.
The paper goes back to detailing the forsaken
events of the day; the flowers on the wallpaper
return to their endless pattern; and the room's
air that had barely quickened seems dustier
as if it had been breathed too long, or
for too long had been unmoving and unchanged.

Letter Beginning with the First Line of Your Letter

Here the weather remains the same. Constant
summer sun. When was the sky anything but blue?
In the harbor park, boys on bikes plague lovers
and the pink-eyed dogs of the elderly.
Across the water, freighters take on cargo.
I stand on the shore, envying each destination.
Because you are not here, I think of you
everywhere; wherever they are going
they must be going to you. We were like
fat people in old cartoons who could
barely kiss for all their mortal baggage;
like holiday travelers who have missed their trains,
are stranded in a European station surrounded by
wicker baskets, belted trunks. We had such baggage.
It increased and became such a mountain that we
lost each other behind it, until our voices
grew distant and we returned to writing letters.
Whose baggage, whose mistakes, who cares now?
Listen, I am thirty-six, I have lived in
many cities and within me it is raining.
The deliberate ocean repeats and repeats.
Empty life-guard stands, paper cups and
plastic spoons, the folded green cabanas—
all mark the deserted beaches of the heart.
Water drips from colored pennants, glistens
on the black taxis on the esplanade.
In the empty ballroom of a beach hotel, someone
is practising the piano. In sitting rooms and parlors,
guests turn the pages of their magazines, look at
rain on window panes, look at watches, look at

the closed door of a dining room from which they hear
the rattle of dishes and silver, of tables being set.
Listen, from such a place I am writing you a letter.
Again and again, I try to put down a few words.
As day and sky dissolve in sheets of gray,
the sea repeats your name to the desireless sand.

Snow

I

The tree you reached for when you started
to fall, the house you wrapped around you: all
the surfaces you leaned against were lessened
in the night, and today's snow is a layer
of yesterday's dependable world stripped clean.
The air fills with white movement like
the inside of a wall or a movie screen when
the film snaps and you still search for patterns
within the white flickering. Wind scrapes the earth
like a man rubbing a stain from his sleeve, confusing
earth and sky, heaping barriers before you until
you stop, jarred from that sequence of moments
you call your life, and alone on the street,
encumbered by deep snow, you become like someone
on a window ledge: too frightened to jump,
uncertain how to climb back inside.

2

If your past is the statue of yourself, then
your memories are chips from that statue
and you turn them over, seeking the beginnings
of a pattern. If today's cold is like drapery
or liquid, covering all it touches, then cold
remembered becomes tangible: the person you
took sledding, who embraced you as you lay
in the snow, catching flakes with your eyes.
But today you are struck by the formlessness
of cold as it tries to insinuate itself into
your clothes, as if it wanted to walk through town
disguised in your body, laying a single transparent
hand against the cheek of each person you pass.
Tomorrow, you will only remember that snow and wind
seemed stonelike: some abstract statue you couldn't
decipher, that you spent hours trying to bypass
in the irregular journey of your day.

3

From the hill, across snow-covered fields, the cars
leaving town at five o'clock seem as one body of light.
The sky has cleared, and in the dark the stars
are sharp white points. You think if you knew
what lines to draw between them, you would
no longer feel so unsettled in this life.
The cars continue in a white stream, lighting up
the snow at the edge of the road; then in groups
of threes and fours they begin to fall away
and dark holes appear in the body of light.
Standing on the hill with the snow deep around you
and the wind like a hand against you, you now see
single points break off into their streets, moving
so slowly they appear to crawl toward the dead ends
of their driveways, and you catch your breath
as one by one each light stops, then goes dark.

4

The man climbing from his car at the edge of town
looks toward his shoveled walk and the yellow light
above his front door, then looks out across fields
of deep snow which the wind tugs in a way he
interprets as impatience. He locks his car door,
then pauses, and briefly all the small losses
of his life come together, the disappointments
solidify, as if he were on a ledge staring down
into his snow-covered life. And turning from his home,
he wants to walk out into the snow and keep walking
until his legs grow stiff and he will lie down
and something will embrace him and all the stars
will come together in one light to warm him.
Now his dog barks and someone calls to him
from his front door, but he takes a few steps
toward the fields and for a moment he hears only
the steady swirl of snow and beneath it a language:
the first words of which he is coming to understand.

Song for Falling Asleep

It is something on the ground, something
in the backyard of a small German village.
You are lying in the bomb bay on the return flight
from Hamburg: too much cloud, too much flak.
From this height it could be a red blanket
on a clothesline, even the top of a red car.
To the pilot it's a rodeo clown waving a flag
at a bull that has just thrown a cowboy. He
was once such a cowboy. The plane circles.
It is the only outlaw in this sky.
In the bomb bay you are nearly asleep.
You think tomorrow you will begin a new poem.
To the bombardier it's the hole made by a .22
that has mistakenly gone off and hit someone
standing nearby, perhaps a younger brother.
He arranges his sights over the bloodmark.
In the bomb bay you listen to a roaring which you
believe is the sound of blood in your veins.
You are lulled by the rushing of wind.
You are weightless and feel you are falling.

Song for Putting Aside Anger

Four walls open to the sky: you are
in a small prison. There is no door.
You are here for hatred, theft; it doesn't
matter. You might have been here all your life.
You might have come yesterday. It feels like
your entire life. It feels like your friends
have all died. You imagine their bodies
in a white room. Perhaps you killed them.
Your throat is too small for your hatred.
You sit sifting dirt through your fingers.
You say it is your heart: a dry sand,
an encumbrance. You wish it were a
red bird in the blue sky above you.

In the hills above you, a dozen monks
hurry along a road toward a mountain.
They wear blue robes. They play flutes and
small cymbals. In the midst of four walls,
you listen to the high notes of the flutes,
the chime of the cymbals. The sounds turn,
spin together in the air around you,
weaving together into a thin rope.
Having found it, you must trust it.
This is how you put aside anger:
pulling yourself up, hand over hand.

Song of Four Dancers

A path between two rows of pines; spring
smell of pine needles and dark earth;
gray stone benches along the path; morning fog—
he remembers her hands which moved like
impatient birds as she spoke. He remembers
the smell of her hair: wood smoke
and pine, and the touch of that hair
spun by some spider king. He remembers
the air that pushed from his lungs.
Some days later she flew to Europe. Twenty
years. Now he tries to imagine her
in one of the world's rooms, eating or
drinking, a life passed among strangers.

At the end of the path, four statues
in green bronze: four women in a shallow pool
dancing with raised arms. The fog breaks;
the sun glitters on the bronze. Kneeling,
she drinks from the pond, water
runs from her cupped fingers. Watching her,
he cannot imagine a time without her.

The Wine Glass

In your hand, the wine glass is breaking,
as yet we don't know it. The sun's last light,
the room with its portraits and brass lamps,
our faces and the faces of our friends—
all move within the shadows of your glass:
a champagne glass, ring of gold around the rim,
a long green stem around which you curve
two fingers. We speak of how people
portray themselves in this hotel of strangers,
of indulgence and the false self. Something
strikes you and you laugh. Without warning
the glass becomes fragments in your hand,
spilling wine down your dress, spreading a stain
over the orange carpet. We stare down as if
listening for some sound or word called across
the summer fields, the freshly mown lawns.
Suddenly a swallow hits the window and drops,
an ounce of feathered trash. We began by saying
goodbye: each greeting contains a farewell.

2

This morning as you sleep, I shape small circles
on the down of your belly. The undulations
of your body, landscape of stomach and breasts—
each blond hair repeats the morning sun
against the tan of your skin. Across the room,
a print of Flemish minstrels becomes a skull
through some trick of light. Two months ago today,
my cousin died in his sleep. The mirror
in front of the bed reflects a picture
behind the bed: a dirt road curving up a hill,
a windmill beside a small farm, November elms
and maples, a flight of birds going away,
a pond where I imagine my cousin has drowned—
I see myself climbing the hill: a journey taken
without sense of beginning or knowledge of end.
Last night as you slept a single bat swooped
and fluttered in figure eights. Darker
than the room in the moon's light, its body
became a hunting vacancy above our bed.

3

My cousin and I were two lines beginning
at the same point, then diverging. As children
we'd been close. He was best at departures—
a pick-up or car backing down the black top.
He chose his friends among the old and retired.
They met at a camp in the woods to discuss
what had happened to who and why. Now, as they
gather in green workclothes, he fills their mouths.
He retired early, still as a child. We said
he had seen nothing. He saw all he wanted.
Dead at thirty-five, he avoided his middle years
and died an old man, having refused the journey.
As we carried his coffin through a narrow door,
it tilted, began to slip: a moment my cousin
would have liked had he been there. Although May,
it snowed in the night. Wet snow surrounded
the flowers, striped tent, entrance to the earth.
As children, we stole similar flowers to decorate
a shack we'd built in the woods: dirt floor,
tarpaper roof, privacy as fragile as silence.

4

It's not my cousin's death before me now.
Last night at dinner each face contained a crack
which during the meal widened and narrowed
in response to the faces around it. They weren't
children or particularly fragile. Earlier
that day we looked out from a hill overlooking
Washington County while on the lake below us
small figures water-skied or lay around
as we did in the afternoon sun. To the east
the Green Mountains were the edge of a wave.
In the woods, a squirrel rustled in dead leaves
or a farmer's son crept forward with a knife
or camera. Surrounded by the lawful day, we
wrenched an hour out of sequence. Clouds shifted
across the sun's blank face. Slowly our own faces
exploded into each other, fragments of bare skin,
parts of our bodies flung across green fields,
tumbling in a landslide of maple and pine
toward darkening water, sailor drowned.

5

The morning sun moves across your sleeping face.
A month ago you didn't exist; in a few days
you are going away. My thumb traces a road
along the inside of your thigh. Already
in our voices are the edges which with time
will become sharper. We move from ignorance
to awareness, acceptance to doubt.
Lying beside you, I ease my cousin's coffin
through the chapel door. You and I met
like people on the back steps of passing trains:
your face recedes in the distance, a little death.
Each night at dinner, surrounded by strangers,
we speak of the dead, eat and drink of the dead.
In living faces are small deaths of embarrassment,
intolerance, contempt. Touch your face:
touch your skull. Last night after dinner,
I gave you wine in a green stemmed glass.
The last sun caught in your hair, reflected
in the red wine of the glass just then ready
to shatter in your scarcely more permanent hand.

Geese

As a green thread winds through blue fabric
so this morning the sound of geese weaves
through the border of blue sky. He turns
past oak and maple gone golden, but sees only
a single crow heading north. In the pasture,
a man on horseback pursues three black steers.

In his dream it was a different house
and his friends were older: their faces
like fragments of bright light. A blue plate
had been broken and he searched among
the pieces, trying to put them together.
Through the window he saw the colors
of late summer. A feeling of falling:
then something touched his arm. Light filled
the doorway and he seemed to lean against it.
These were friends he had not seen for years.

Returning to this town after an absence
of ten years, he keeps seeing himself pass
in cars, duck into stores, gathered with
friends around the tables of houses
he walks by at night. Half the streets
are torn up, half the buildings torn down.
He imagines who he might have become had he stayed.
At a traffic accident, he watches a man
twist on his stomach in the middle of a street:
the side of his face torn like wet paper.
Standing by the curb, he starts to call out,
then hurries away before the man can turn over.

One April in Ontario: a day so gray
that the lowering sky seemed intent
on stroking the earth. The air filled
with the sound of geese, and in wet fields
thousands of geese waddled, quarreled, stared
at the sky as flight after flight swept
over the fence where he stood with his friends:
a pocket of silence that seemed the very center
of the place the geese were coming home to.
That was eight years before and now
such a memory as to be something from a dream,
forgotten in the morning, then recalled
as he walks through the pasture and hears
the sound of geese going away, pausing
without knowing why, feeling a touch
on his arm, turning and finding himself alone.

In Place of a Letter

For an instant I turned from your face to the road
and suddenly you were a thousand miles away.
Think of all the prosthetic devices between us,
all the leg braces and false teeth. To the west I see
mountains of artificial hair, glass eyes of every color.
I try to imagine you on the other side, studying
another sunset. I try to imagine your face:
it is like a reflection in a still pool,
and each day becomes a rock tossed from shore
until you are lost among rough water. Each evening,
as the clouds begin to break apart at sunset
so your face begins to fragment in my memory.
Then each morning I try to rebuild you. I find
gray cloud and say that is the color of your eyes.
In the slope of hills, I see shoulders and breasts.
I tell myself, even if your face is changed I won't
mistake your hair, and I search the spines of my books
for that dark shade of red. Constantly I construct you
from the world around me until it seems I wander
within you without knowing where you are, as if
you were some house I'd built without windows or doors,
as if you were some forest and I were lost within you.

I feel that I move from one town to the next
like a ball rolling down a hill. Why did it move
in the first place? Where is it going? I feel
that each time I change my direction, part of me
gets left behind. I think of the lost teeth, the cut
fragments of hair, the cells that replace themselves
every seven years, the people and stories I've forgotten.
Remembering each departure, it's as if I abandoned
feet in New Jersey, hands in New York. I imagine

being pursued by parts of my body in the same way
scraps of paper seem to pursue a passing truck.
I imagine the parts joining together until someplace
is this duplicate self. But it's not me he'll follow.
He's put together my lost common sense, and now
he's moving west through half the towns between us
until at last you see him at the edge of your lawn.
Speak to him, invite him inside. You will know him
because he will plant seeds, because he is someone
who is not listening for some sound in the distance,
who can hear traffic without twisting in his chair,
because he owns no suitcase, because he has a face
from which nothing is missing, a face with none of
the restlessness of water, the instability of cloud.

Moon Song

I was lonely. I looked
at myself in the mirror.
My reflection was lonely.
I found Scotch tape and
taped my face to the mirror:
round yellow face in a dark room.
I took the mirror outside
along with my shotgun and one shell.
Warm September night. I greeted
familiar constellations. Nothing
had fallen. Imitating old statues,
I sailed the mirror into the sky.
Before it fell, I raised the shotgun
and shot. Not for nothing
was I rifle club president.
Now in my living room, I glance
casually from the window. It's been
a long evening: nothing on the TV,
nothing in my books. Boy, I'd sure
be lonely if it weren't for that big
yellow face up there counting stars.

The Poem As Actor In Three Parts For
Michael Ryan

I

The poem sits on a bench at the local stop when the express roars through. The third car is full of its audience and seeing the poem they wave. But the poem is deep in a book and does no more than raise its little finger. At the sight of the finger, a pregnant woman at the end of the platform feels her water break and later that day she gives birth to twin boys who she names, inexplicably, T.S. and Nicanor. Her husband, a maker of arch supports, sobs through the night, but by morning has decided to leave home and, like Rimbaud, seek his fortune selling guns to the King of Abyssinia.

2

I have some friends who fashioned a love doll out of three poems— one by Yeats— and left it outside Michael Ryan's house. When Michael came out, he was so moved by the poetry he didn't see it was an inflatable doll and he asked it or rather her inside which in any case was where it or rather she was going. Well, my friends waited and after a few minutes there was an explosion and Michael came sailing out the window like a pink rocket. What harm could he come to? To my friends' surprise, Michael landed on his feet and strolled off whistling: so great is his love of poetry.

3

This poem which appears to be on the page is actually on an ice floe in the Bering Sea sharpening its harpoon. Far out to sea, its audience is gathered in a protoplasmic mass. They are so nervous and tense that they accidentally shoot a stream of water up through a hole in their head. Seeing this, the poem jumps in its kayak and begins to paddle. The audience swims off, full of terror and self-recrimination. The sun is high in the sky; the poem paddles. The sun sets; the poem paddles. Now it is dark; the poem paddles faster.

Arrested Saturday Night

This is how it happened: Peg and Bob had invited
Jack and Roxanne over to their house to watch
the TV, and on the big screen they saw Peg and Bob,
Jack and Roxanne watching themselves watch
themselves on progressively smaller TVs. Outside
it was autumn. Strips of cloud brushed the moon.
Also outside a prowler stood under the big maple
in the front yard, and he didn't see the moon, nor
hear formations of geese crossing the night sky.
Instead he watched Peg and Bob and their guests
watching themselves watch themselves on the TV. And
also outside, in a white Pontiac parked at the curb,
the policeman didn't feel winter approaching, nor smell
smoke from where kids had burned leaves for quarters.
Instead he watched the prowler watch the people
watching themselves on the TV, and he saw all this
through the big front window of his big car, itself
a kind of screen, which I can easily swear to since I
saw everything through the picture window of my house
across the street, and I was kicking the wall and
hammering on the glass not because my Doberman had
gone rabid, nor because my air conditioner was pumping out
yellow smoke, nor because I believe that television
is the closest mechanical approximation of death
available to man, no, I was hammering because the audio
was broken on my picture window, and with all that silence
and useless staring, well, shit, I'd had it up to here.

Separations

I

To begin with photographs of summer: lakes
ringed by white birch held by hands of white bone—
skeletons as delicate as the skeletons of birds.
To begin with a scene in a theater: a man and
woman sit on a red couch and between them
are photographs so bright that each becomes
a small lamp lighting their faces, making
a circle of yellow light around the couch;
but then it is darker, and moving back one sees
that the couch is alone on an empty stage.
The man and woman look at the photographs
and although they are talking there is no sound.
The only sound comes from a cleaning woman
at the back of the theater as she moves along
each row. She is old and lives with her cat.
She thinks of nothing but raising the seats
which she likes to flick up in such a way
that each snaps shut. Outside it is snowing and
almost dark. People hurry from office to home.
They are dissatisfied and all their cars
complain: snarling, honking, hating each other.

2

We sit in a parked car on an empty street
and I keep trying to talk but everything
in the car is shouting: the steering wheel
and dashboard, the pedals and black vinyl seats—
all keep shouting. Now your hands are pressed
against your ears and I keep raising my voice.
Cold night, cold street, rows of dark apartments—
then I see a gray dog run into an alley
carrying some creature in its mouth, something
that twists and raises its arms. And raising
my arms I turn toward you and abruptly
the shouting stops and the place where you were
sitting fills with silence. Before I can speak,
soften my words, you jump from the car.
Once, when you were away for a week, I wrote
your name on a banner to welcome you home.
Now the wind blows pieces of paper against
the car windows, and on each I see a letter
of your name, as if my voice were a pair of hands
good for nothing but tearing and breaking. How
did we become so foreign? I tell myself, I could
collect these fragments, patch them together.
I sit without moving as wind rocks my car,
whips scraps of white paper through the street.

3

A man and woman are being rowed out to sea.
Curved blades of gray water cut the bottom
of gray sky. She wears a red scarf and a thick
gray cloak. Their faces are red with cold.
He holds her hand, but through their heavy gloves
they feel nothing. Snow drifts down into the water
around them. With each wave, the boat lifts up,
then settles back farther from land. Their eyes
have not yet left the land: a yellow field
over which the sun is setting. On the shore,
a man and woman embrace, standing as one figure.
She wears a red scarf. They watch the couple
become smaller through snow and gathering night
until there is nothing but a red fleck on the shore,
until there is nothing but darkness and the steady
creaking of oars, until all they can see is a single
white gull where the scarf had been, weaving
back and forth on the night air like a hand.

4

I enter a room with a woman I can't
remember meeting. There is no furniture
and our feet clatter on the wood floor.
It is clear we will live here, that we will
begin furnishing this room and the house
that must surround it. Then there is a noise
at the window, and glancing up I see a bird
pressed between the glass and the dark night
behind it: wings fluttering on the pane,
claws making a scratching noise against
the hard surface. It rises, then falls back.
Behind it, tall pines struggle in the wind.
My love, the bird has your face. Its mouth
opens and closes. Its face is twisted
as if a hand within its body were squeezing,
like squeezing a piece of soft bread. I see
tears on its cheeks, and it seems to be
calling out, although I hear only the squeak
of claws on glass. The woman beside me
looks toward the window. What is it, she
asks, what is it? How can I begin to tell her
of our years together? I catch my breath and
wait and soon I will tell her it is nothing.
Cold night, cold street: my love, we had such
kind intentions.

It's Like This

for P.P.

Each morning the man rises from bed because the invisible
    cord leading from his neck to someplace in the dark,
    the cord that makes him always dissatisfied,
    has been wound tighter and tighter until he wakes.

He greets his family, looking for himself in their eyes,
    but instead he sees shorter or taller men, men with
    different degrees of anger or love, the kind of men
    that people who hardly know him often mistake
    for him, leaving a movie or running to catch a bus.

He has a job that he goes to. It could be at a bank
    or a library or turning a piece of flat land
    into a ditch. All day something that refuses to
    show itself hovers at the corner of his eye,
    like a name he is trying to remember, like
    expecting a touch on the shoulder, as if someone
    were about to embrace him, a woman in a blue dress
    whom he has never met, would never meet again.
    And it seems the purpose of each day's labor
    is simply to bring this mystery to focus. He can
    almost describe it, as if it were a figure at the edge
    of a burning field with smoke swirling around it
    like white curtains shot full of wind and light.

When he returns home, he studies the eyes of his family to see
    what person he should be that evening. He wants to say:
    All day I have been listening, all day I have felt
    I stood on the brink of something amazing.
    But he says nothing, and his family walks around him
    as if he were a stick leaning against a wall.

Late in the evening the cord around his neck draws him to bed.
He's consoled by the coolness of sheets, pressure
of blankets. He turns to the wall, and as water
drains from a sink so his daily mind slips from him.
Then sleep rises before him like a woman in a blue dress,
and darkness puts its arms around him, embracing him.
Be true to me, it says, each night you belong to me more,
until at last I lift you up and wrap you within me.

A Place in Maine

Shoebox upon shoebox— the elderly dawdle
at the backs of rooms; the middle-aged lean
from windows; the young rush in and out, in and out,
while cars collide like the applause of metal gloves.
All morning in my shoebox I try to write about a man
who moved from Connecticut to southern Maine,
bought a crumbling Coast Guard tower and now spends
entire weeks with a telescope staring east.
But each time I put down a word, a train
runs over it; each time a thought flutters
to the edge of my mind, a siren pins it
to its own black page. Each time I imagine
this man from Connecticut seeking truth by hunting
just in one place I hear a malevolent suit of armor
trample the cars, jostle the buildings, reach
into apartments and shout into ears that are like
dried flowers, like porcelain; and as I think of
this man I don't care if he finds truth or that
every day his wife and kids row back and forth
his limited patch of water with signs saying:
George is unfair and George is a creep.
I only imagine how quiet it must be in that tower
with the gulls crying of loss and violation
and the ocean slapping the beach to keep it breathing.
Outside, the mayor of this city is breaking bottles.
Outside, they have lined up ambulances,
fire trucks, police cars and remembering a sound
that once moved them, they try to play Beethoven.
Outside the dogs reproduce their small replicas
of Rodin's Thinker, and pigeons hurl themselves
against the wall across the street because they know
the quick crack of their necks snaps my attention

from Kittery, Maine, where George stares out past
his wife and kids with signs and sense of betrayal,
stares east looking for and why shouldn't he find it:
some black freighter or Flying Dutchman; and George,
look, look, what's that pressing through the fog,
what's that raft of pine logs with two figures—
a tall woman in white with her hand on the head
of a huge Siberian tiger. Now they turn toward you
and both look so wise and benevolent that you're
sorry your wife isn't by your side so you could
take her arm and say: Hey, Honey! Hey, look at this!
Ah, George, the whole damn thing's a lie.
This is Boston, December, 1978. Now winter
sticks its hard body up the cracks of this city
and all my world is busting up outside.

Pablo Neruda

Pablo Neruda stands on a corner next to a poster
advertising quick weight loss diet aids when I
happen by with half my creative writing class.
He wears a black boating cap and blue cloak draped
loosely over one shoulder, and he stands very still
staring at the clouds where he probably sees the profiles
of famous poets. At his feet lies a small brown dog.
We had heard he was dead and so are surprised and
walk around him several times. He has nice fat cheeks
and after a moment I reach out and touch one, but
gently and he doesn't notice. I look at my students
and I can tell they're ready for anything so I
take out my Swiss army knife, open the littlest
blade and cut Pablo a tiny bit on the left arm.
He doesn't even blink but I think he begins to
concentrate more intently on the clouds. By now
my students are becoming excited so I open a bigger
blade and carefully cut a sliver of flesh from his
shoulder. I put it on my tongue and it's very sweet
with a faint taste of smoke. I chew it slowly.
Glancing at the sky it now seems a deeper blue.
My students see me smiling and licking my lips
and they too take out Swiss army knives and start
cutting off small slices, although they don't stay
small for long, because suddenly we are ravenous.
It feels like I haven't eaten for days. I barely
pause to chew my food and I grow angry at my students
for pushing and getting aggressive over the more
succulent bits. One even eats the brown dog.
In practically no time there's nothing left but
a quickly folded pile of clothes on the sidewalk
with the black cap on top. Then we all become

embarrassed and won't look at each other because
we've eaten this famous poet, and even though he
tasted great and we could probably eat another,
and even though the city seems brighter and more
exciting than before, we still feel ashamed to have
surrendered so completely to such animal passions
so we point to our watches and make excuses and
stroll off in our separate directions, but shortly,
outside a movie theater, I see one of my students
offering herself to the people waiting in line;
then I see another accosting a crowd at a bus stop;
and a little later in the lobby of a convention hotel
I see a third bothering the legionnaires. And you,
now that I have your attention at last, ignore these
imposters. They're too hungry to be telling the truth.
Feel this arm, this fat thigh. Why would I cheat you?
Even now the moon grows more swollen and the stars
throb deep in their black pockets. Bite me, bite me!

Song of Basic Necessities

The day hates you and the wind has stolen
the coat from your back. Take this poem.
Unfolding it from the page, it becomes a cloak.
Now as you walk through the streets of winter,
you listen idly to the talk of the unfaithful:
how you must have flattered the sun
for it to give you a ray to wrap around you.

You are hungry and haven't eaten for days:
the food of the world becomes ash in your mouth.
Take this poem. Now it is a banquet: wine, fish,
freshly baked bread. You invite your friends
to a clearing by the river. Just as you fear there
won't be enough, more food appears and the glasses
refill themselves like the feast in another story.

You are lost and without shelter. People
avoid you, storms seek you out. Take this poem.
It is a tent to put around you. Warm within it,
you prepare for sleep, while in the rushing
of the wind you now hear the voices
of your friends. They speak of their love for you.
They hope tomorrow you will come home.

Song of the Wrong Response

The poem is barechested, black and
shadowboxing beneath a streetlight.
In the rest of the city it is dark.
You're out walking your dog. Nervously,
you circle the poem. It turns toward you
and speaks of a disease of the heart,
perhaps anger. You can't make out the words.
Never have you seen a face so ugly. Then
it steps toward you and swings. You jump.
Still, it strikes you once above the heart.
On the sidewalk your dog is asleep. The poem
returns to shadowboxing. You are that exciting.
Once home, you phone the proper authorities.
Then I arrive and you describe the attack.
All next day you look at mugshots before finding
the right picture: a young man with some flowers.
This, I say, is a poem about love and
the difficulties of friendship. It is about
reaching out in dark places. The poem
touched you above the heart and you fled.
What happened in fact, you have forgotten.
What happened in memory will repeat itself and
each time you will act falsely and be afraid.

The Delicate, Plummeting Bodies

A great cry went up from the stockyards and
slaughterhouses, and Death, tired of complaint
and constant abuse, withdrew to his underground garage.
He was still young and his work was a torment.
All over, their power cut, people stalled like street cars.
Their gravity taken away, they began to float.
Without buoyancy, they began to sink. Each person
became a single darkened room. The small hand
pressed firmly against the small of their backs
was suddenly gone and people swirled to a halt
like petals fallen from a flower. Why hurry?
Why get out of bed? People got off subways,
on subways, off subways all at the same stop.
Everywhere clocks languished in antique shops
as their hands composed themselves in sleep.
Without time and decay, people grew less beautiful.
They stopped eating and began to study their feet.
They stopped sleeping and spent weeks following stray dogs.
The first to react were remnants of the church.
They falsified miracles: displayed priests posing
as corpses until finally they sneezed or grew lonely.
Then governments called special elections to choose those
to join the ranks of the volunteer dead: unhappy people
forced to sit in straight chairs for weeks at a time.
Interest soon dwindled. Then the army seized power
and soldiers ran through the street dabbling the living
with red paint. You're dead, they said. Maybe
tomorrow, people answered, today we're just breathing:
look at the sky, look at the color of the grass.
For without Death each color had grown brighter.
At last a committee of businessmen met together,
because with Death gone money had no value.

They went to where Death was waiting in a white room,
and he sat on the floor and looked like a small boy
with pale blond hair and eyes the color of clear water.
In his lap was a red ball heavy with the absence of life.
The businessmen flattered him. We will make you king,
they said. I am king already, Death answered. We will
print your likeness on all the money of the world.
It is there already, Death answered. We adore you
and will not live without you, the businessmen said.
Death said, I will consider your offer.

How Death was restored to his people:

At first the smallest creatures began to die—
bacteria and certain insects. No one noticed. Then fish
began to float to the surface; lizards and tree toads
toppled from sun-warmed rocks. Still no one saw them.
Then birds began tumbling out of the air,
and as sunlight flickered on the blue feathers
of the jay, brown of the hawk, white of the dove,
then people lifted their heads and pointed to the sky
and from the thirsty streets cries of welcome rose up
like a net to catch the delicate and plummeting bodies.

The Invisibles

for Isabel Bize

> *"The term Wärmestod (heat death) gives the picture of the hot stars of the universe heating up the dark areas of the universe until everything comes to a uniform temperature and a final state of maximum universal entropy is reached."*
> Norman Dolloff, *Heat Death and the Phoenix*

I

He has crawled on his belly across six lanes
of highway and now straddles the guard rail
as if he could ride it away. Cars once more
begin to move; tires passing within inches of
one foot. September morning, blue sky, long strip
of park between the river and Storrow Drive.
You were passing on your bike. The man looks up
from his place on the rail as you ride by. He looks
like a brush used to clean industrial chimneys:
from shoes to cap one shade of carbon gray.
Place a diamond in a furnace and it begins to
turn to graphite. You think of the necklaces
ready to change to lead pencil, the constant
tilt toward disorder. The man heaves a leg
over the rail. He is your age. You imagine him
thirty years ago, sitting in a classroom,
clean-faced and learning to put down words.

2

It seemed all night you were kept awake by hot,
    windless air that pressed itself around you
    like those repeated questions about details
    of your future; kept awake by sirens that
    tore sleep the way you tear sheets of paper;
    kept awake by men from a nearby gay bar
    quarreling in the street: the sound of running
    and someone shouting—Jimmy, you know I love you,
    I've got to kill you. Then the sound of shooting.

It seemed all night you examined yourself as a boy
    examines his back yard: here were green bits
    of glass by the edge of a fence, here something
    fat and prickly found under a rock. It seemed each
    possible path into your future ended in disorder,
    like a painting returning itself to tubes of paint
    or gold rings becoming so much gravel in a stream.
    It seemed you were drifting apart like smoke blown
    from the mouth of a primitive god, and you
    imagined a fat black god in a jungle clearing
    surrounded by rituals of futility and slaughter.

3

Your students fall naturally into rows: four down,
six across, a model of crystalline structure; and
although you urge them to form a rough circle
actually it pleases you to see them mapped and
manageable. They are here to learn different ways
of arranging words in sequence. You tell them
about the man who crawled across Storrow Drive,
not sure why it remains in your mind. Some say
they've seen him, others have seen ones like him:
all that same carbon gray like mortar chipped out
from the crevices around brick.
                          After class, you
return to your office to try to write a letter.
You want to articulate your sense of the imminent
dissolution of your life, but all you can find
are metaphors of absence. But because you are
trying to set down words, someplace else words
are crumbling like a muddy hillside during rain,
someplace else words are being shouted at random.
Because you are thinking, someplace else a mind
is falling into silence. Because you are sitting,
someplace a man is running. Because you are
temporarily at rest, he feels afraid. He is
running without thought and feels afraid.

4

My friend, in the weeks you've been gone,
your face and body, the sound of your voice,
have become like January fog in my mind.
I touch what is left of you like touching
a window in a warm room. Outside it is winter.
The trees are limp and withdrawn. I think of
the waste of such days spent without you,
the pointlessness of another pointless move,
as if there were actually directions, directions
to be found. Here the city spends its days
honing its edges of glass and steel, and I
think if I could treat my mind likewise; if
I could assemble it as a child fabricates order
with an erector set of bolts and tin girders,
then I might possibly exclude the thought of you.
Right now you sweep through my mind like
wind through a tent: no keeping you there,
no keeping you out.

5

This morning from the moment of waking
you felt accompanied by a shadow self
that no amount of thought would draw closer
or drive away. You sense that as you become
weaker and more distraught, it gains in substance,
and were this to continue you would change places
and it would pick up the stray ends of your life,
while you trailed behind: a bit of cloth in a wind.
But you realize that even for it the questions
would accumulate, as with someone on a beach
picking up stones, and that soon it would begin
to lose the substance it took from you, just as you,
temporarily free of questions, became less shadow;
and you would again change places and immediately
the eternal why of it would begin chipping away
and the questions would again accumulate until
you became as burdened as a man forced to carry
stone after stone for some wall or stone house—
the constant construction of an incomplete life.

6

In Copley Square, the derelicts sit side by side
on a stone bench. This one snaps and bites the air.
This one wears white spats and holds a black umbrella
between himself and blue sky. This one talks happily
to the empty place beside him as if talking
to someone he's known all his life. Those others—
their opposites, the sleek ones in bright colors
who the city names successful— they keep
crossing the square and the derelicts keep trying
to catch their attention, not just for money or
conversation, but to prove themselves visible;
but they remain unsuccessful and nobody pauses.
Let's burn one. Let's stop fooling around and simply
burn one. Let's collect the carbon-colored clothes,
make a pile, light it and toss one on. Say,
the one with the umbrella or the one talking
to his friend the silence. Then the fire department
comes rushing up with five pieces of equipment
and they'll rush into the square and rush around but
they won't see anything, and one of the bums
will holler: There's a guy burning up on top of a pile
of our good coats. But the firemen won't see him.
Just another false alarm, they'll say and rush home.
Maybe there's one burning right now. Maybe
that's what the one bum is saying, the one
snapping and biting the air. Maybe he's trying
to tell you about the black smoke which you're
too dumb to see and his good friend, another bum,
blazing up on a stack of old coats in Copley Square.

7

Upstairs in the library reading room, you think
of the epitaph of the acrobat in the Roman
amphitheater in southern France: He danced, he died.
And you envy that without understanding it.
You think of how the dance means giving up heat
and how giving up heat means death. And you
are unwilling to accept that. You tell yourself
in a fire nothing is destroyed; the molecules
of the Van Gogh painting are replaced by slightly
different molecules of ash and smoke. And you
feel yourself caught within that sense of value
as if locked in a small white room. He danced,
he died. You look around the reading room with its
statues of famous thinkers and long tables and
dozens of men and women tunneling themselves into
the books lying open before them. You imagine
beginning to twist and spin down the main aisle,
frightened by the violence of your own dance
as you start kicking the green glass shades
of the reading lamps, kicking the stone busts of
famous writers, ruffling the hair of the readers,
snatching their hats, tossing their books across
the oak tables, making them get up and chase you
from one side of the room to the other until
you break through the stained glass window,
break out of the library into the air above
Copley Square, where you imagine you can fly.

Later, taking the subway back to Kenmore Square,
you watch the people staring at the spaces
between each other as if filling the gaps
with invisible objects of their desire. Most
carry bags and parcels as if their purchases
were small anchors holding them to the earth.
You realize that you too are carrying such bags—
a record, some books— and you come to see yourself
as some fat balloon, while your objects, your ideas
of how to live, your years in school— all become
like ropes tying you to the earth, ropes which keep
breaking, must be replaced by new ideas and objects;
that without them you would drift into space and
you are terrified by the sense of that black immensity.
At each stop you see derelicts asleep on benches.
You again think that in a fire nothing is destroyed.
You again think of the acrobat: he danced, he died.
But you cannot reconcile the fact of dissolution
with the fact of the dance. It hardly matters: books
mean nothing, the years in school mean nothing, and
the ropes keep breaking. You feel yourself pressed
harder and harder against the ceiling of the car
and you try to imagine what your own place will be
when you are no longer held down to this earth.
Shortly, the train reaches Kenmore Square;
you hurry to your office afraid and without thought.

8

My friend, today I feel if I touched the people
around me, my hand would pass through them.
Either they are cloud or I am shadow—
it makes no difference. Today I feel
the parts of myself fly outward until it seems
even my love for you is being pried from me.
Think of it as a child in a red coat. Think of
that child on a flat acre of woods and the whole
acre pried and cut from the earth like a table top.
Think of that table top flung into space,
that acre of woods spinning off in great circles,
slowly becoming smaller as the child races
dizzily to each tree, say, a stand of white birch,
and the entire acre of birch and child with it
disappearing into darkness like a dime down a well.
Down here my world falls to disorder and even
the seasons become confused. Down here
it is now winter and night presses upon me.
The pines in their great coats of snow
shuffle a few steps closer to the house.

9

When two bodies are in thermal balance, no
heat passes from one to the other.
                          A man in
a small room tries to order his thoughts which
flick away like water flicked from the hands.
The air around his body is slightly warmer
than the chill air of the room.
                          Energy cannot
be created or destroyed. In an isolated system,
the amount of energy is constant. The energy
of the universe is constant.
                          A man pushes himself
through deep snow while the wind swirls
more snow around him. The warmth of his
body melts a few flakes as his own body
temperature falls.
                          All natural processes
move in a direction that leads to equilibrium.
The flow of heat is always from the higher to
lower temperature. The entropy of the universe
strives to a maximum.
                          A man hurries down a
hallway with green cinderblock walls. The lights
are spaced some yards apart and the man runs
from light to dark, light to dark. He is afraid
and runs without conscious thought. Where is
he going? He is already there.
                          At absolute zero,
the entropy of a perfect crystal is zero.

10

You are tired and your body feels heavy.
All afternoon you've stayed in your office
elaborating questions. You feel your body
surrender itself to the air around it, and you're
tired of simply accepting that, of watching
your body decrease itself to no purpose.
Now, as you bicycle back, Storrow Drive is
jammed with five o'clock traffic, a constant
roar erasing and obliterating all sound.
To your left the brown water of the river
turns golden in the light of the setting sun
which also colors the surfaces of cars,
changing the traffic into long strings of jewelry.
You think of the derelict you rode by that morning,
and reaching the park in front of the band shell
you see him on the empty stage, facing the grass
where two boys toss a baseball. The derelict stands
nearly at the lip of the stage with his arms
out-stretched, and at first you think he's in pain,
but then you realize he is singing, although
you hear nothing over the noise of traffic.
The boys playing ball don't seem to notice.
The joggers passing in a steady stream don't look up.
The man takes a step forward, charcoal gray from
cap to foot, his mouth gaping in a pink gash
as he concludes his song, arms held as if
to include the park and everything beyond.
As you watch, he seems to become the only
immovable object, while the park and river,
the city itself, begin to revolve around him,

begin to gather speed and spin faster with
this derelict at the very center, the one point
of equilibrium, while the world radiates out
from him in an elaborate skeletal structure.
Even the noise of the traffic becomes the noise
of the gyroscope whirling through space until
you reach out to a tree to steady yourself
and try to look at this derelict who stays gray
even in the sun's last light, but he hurts
your eyes and you turn away, your mind now trying
to locate its place on the body of the gyroscope.
And you decide that wherever you are it must be
at some opposite place; that if he's the tip,
then you're out there in space with nothing to
hold onto, out there tumbling through the dark.
You turn away to where the sun sets red and silent
over the river, and you think of approaching that sun
as one traveling through space. You think of
the roar it must make as gases and flame
flicker and leap thousands of miles. Again
you feel tired, your mind and body feel tired,
and you imagine the final sense of submission
and release as you tumble through space,
your fragmented body a mindless black cinder,
drawn steadily faster toward the arcing fire,
the welcoming flame of the sun's white thunder.

Stephen Dobyns

Stephen Dobyns was born in Orange, New Jersey, in 1941, and raised in New Jersey, Michigan, Virginia and Pennsylvania. He was educated at Shimer College, Wayne State University and The University of Iowa. He has taught at various colleges, including Boston University, The University of Iowa and The University of New Hampshire; and has worked as a reporter for *The Detroit News*. His first book of poems, *Concurring Beasts*, was the Lamont Poetry Selection for 1971. His second book of poems, *Griffon*, appeared in 1976. He has also published two novels: *A Man Of Little Evils* (1973) and *Saratoga Longshot* (1976). He currently teaches in the MFA-Writing Program at Goddard College and lives, with his wife and son, in Searsport, Maine.